The Broads, 1919

Latymer, Hugh Burdett Money-Coutts, Baron

bibliolife

old books. new life.

THE BROADS
1919
BY
HUGH MONEY-COUTTS

WITH A FRONTISPIECE BY DONALD MAXWELL

LONDON: JOHN LANE, THE BODLEY HEAD, W.
NEW YORK: JOHN LANE COMPANY. MCMXX

NOTE

THE following is an explanation of some of the Norfolk terms used in the poem :

Largesse = alms.

Tempest = thunderstorm.

Staithe = quay, or built-up bank.

THE BROADS, 1919

Then Arms were stayed ; and Armistice gave birth
To Peace. Next, all men clamoured for clean mirth
—Innocent joys they loved in bygone days,
Before they trod the unfamiliar ways
Of battle and murder, wounds, and sudden death.
'Twas ended. Many a weary man drew breath
Vowing that his should be a golden year
Of sober joy, and holiday, with fear
Cast out. " Whate'er betide to-morrow,
This happy summer will I beg, or borrow,
Or steal a guerdon from Fate's doubtful store,
And happy live, as once we lived of yore."

At Wroxham all the Wherry folk abide ;
And there, in August, by the waterside
Gathered my venturers. The iron rail
Brought Jim, his sire, and many a box and bale
By God's good mercy, Armistice reprieved
Jim's scanty years ; although in secret grieved
All proper lads, whose age was yet too tender
For sacrifice, full eager to surrender
Their all for England. Summers seventeen
His swiftly questing, eager eyes had seen.

Shadows grew longer; down the dusty road
With whirring wheels drew near a laughing load
Of travellers, a joyous, noisy band.
" Now quickly, Sandy, Gordon, bear a hand;
From your luxurious eyrie rouse you both
And stow the gear," cries Jim; they, nothing
    loath,
Explored the *Endeavour*, opened all the lockers,
While Patience skipped about in knickerbockers.
She was a roly-poly thing to tickle,
O'erflowing with laughter—such a romping pickle,
My nine-year maiden. Sandy was a lad
Could learn from books, and gave the best he had
To scholarship; yet loved to play at cricket,
Trundling a likely ball to take a wicket.
Gordon, long years ago, had almost crossed
Life's borderland; and something he had lost,
And something gained from that far journeying.
Surely an angel with his flaming wing
Had touched him lightly; all too sensitive
He seemed, to live the life which boys should live
Ere manhood dawns; but then for recompense
He was endowed with every artist sense
And sympathy; for him the golden day

10

Was all too short, and oft-times he would stay,
Pencil or brush in hand, till shadowy night
Curtained the earth from his reluctant sight.

Evening drew on; the mother of my flock
Said to her spouse: " Now have we taken stock
Of every tin and bottle; all is done
As orderly as may be. Jim, my son,
'Tis time for supper, lay the cabin table."
Each helped amain, as he or she was able,
And from the fare which heaped the groaning
     board
With conscious virtue claimed a just reward.

That night they slept but ill, for many a midge
Shrills out his spiteful tune by Wroxham bridge,
Blaring his tiny trumpet in defiance
And fierce contempt for Muscatol's appliance.
But when the rosy Dawn from underground
Softly appeared, and drowsily unwound
The earth from darkness, all our Argonauts
Poked out their tousled heads from various ports,
Pleased that the wakeful hours had gone their way
To oblivion in the gulfs of yesterday.

Then on a Sabbath morn they set their sail
Right early, lest the gentle breeze should fail,
Leaving them helpless to the biting gnat
And mordant midge; the timorous water-rat
Scarce marked their passage as they glided by,
Scarce could the ungainly hern their wake descry,
Yet moved they on. Ted, by the idle helm
With wrinkled brow, as one whom cares o'erwhelm,
Turned a reproachful eye towards the trees
Whose leafy screen betrayed the wandering breeze.
Ted—to be sure a careful worthy man—
Was built by Nature to a gloomy plan.
But cookster Dick, save when a tooth did pester
Was ever blithe and merry as a jester.
'Twas such a day when Phœbus gives no quarter;
So, to elude him, in the wine-dark water
Each boy in turn was towed upon a cable,
Or swimming cheerily was well-nigh able
To pace the wherry; and if truth be told,
E'en though the *Endeavour* had a heart of gold,
Her legs were made of lead; for if the wind
Should urge her gently, at a gait resigned,
Sedate, like some old tramp upon the road,
She shuffled on; but if the tempest's goad

12

Pricked her fat sides, she spurned the weather bank,
And where her bows should be, behold, her flank !

Ere dusk, Ted moored the ship by Horning Ferry ;
They ate their meat ; dim craft beyond the wherry
Beguiled the starry night with cheerful noise
And happy laughter ; from astern, the boys
Cast loose the dinghy, clattering all the gear,
And lightly argued who should row, who steer,
Which way to set their course, upstream or down,
And where the ferry lay, and where the town.
With tuneful bickering they pulled away ;
Their fresh young voices in a roundelay
Of eager mirth stole cheerly o'er the tide.
The Harvest Moon uprose, and far and wide
She flung her silvery arrows at the night,
Flaunting her radiant panoply, bedight
With borrowed plumes, but unabashed ; a jade,
But ah ! how lovely, tender ; ne'er dismayed,
She knows her lovers, though she wax or wane,
Shall mark her beauty at the full again.

Next morn the sky was grey. " 'Tis my belief

There's wind a-comin', best take in a reef,"
Said careful Ted. Clink-clank, the ratchet went,
Clink-clank ; Dick to the windlass handle bent
His brawny back, the gaff crept up the mast,
Till Ted sang out : " 'Tis high enough, make fast."
They tied the reef points 'neath the murmuring sail,
Then showed their prudent canvas to the gale.
'Twas but a summery storm, yet sped they quick
Past Horning Hall, to where St. Benedick
His Abbey ruins are ; for rough King Hal
Bethought him how the monks held festival
By the fat banks of Bure, and confiscate
Were all St. Benet's lands ; the Abbey gate
Still lifts a lonely archway—Ichabod
Is written large upon the tumbled sod.

By Acle Bridge they slept ; an aged dame,
Whose brains were nimble, though her legs were lame,
Would sell them fowls, and cabbages. Next day
They lowered the sail, the mast, and pushed their way
Shoulder to quant, with many a heave and groan,
Where sucked the tide beneath the well-worn stone,
Then hoisted sail again ; each quanting pole
Long as the post which marks a Rugby goal,

Was laid in order by the fo'c'sle hatch
Starboard and port ; ready for Dick to snatch
(The wind being foul) in toil to keep his weigh,
So that *Endeavour* should her helm obey
When Ted, main-sheet in hand, hauled in the slack
Before he turned upon the starboard tack.
For, sailing in a narrow water-way,
When well to windward filch what ground you may ;
And, if you are a Norfolk wherry-man,
Down the lee bank you steal what ground you can.

On Stokesby Quay a little ragged boy
Sang : " John, John Barleycorn," and jumped for joy.
" There's few that sings it now, that ancient ditty,"
Said Dick, " for in this war-time, more's the pity,
No yachts nor wherries sailed ; 'twas so the boys
Could win no largesse for their cheerful noise,
And clean forgot the tunes they used to sing,
' John Barleycorn,' and ' Hark, the bells do ring.'"
They threw him pence, and sailed beyond his ken
Into an open land, where reed and fen
Divide the close-cropped meads, and all around
The busy windmills suck the watery ground.
For here the river's bank is built on high,

c

And if the mills should cease to groan and sigh,
The land were drowned. A smiling place indeed
Beneath a summer sky ; for every breed
Of horse and kine spangles the verdant fields
In clustered harmonies, and nature yields
Reluctant tribute to the arts of men.
But if the storms of winter rave, ah ! then
Man shrinks within a scant significance.
His poor devices serve but to enhance
The undying wildness in the windswept earth
And savage skies ; here reigns the wintry dearth
In fear and loneliness, and man must tread
A bitter path to win his daily bread.

And now the spires of Yarmouth town appear ;
And now they shed the sympathetic tear
For certain shipwrecked mariners, whose craft
Gunwhale in mud, sticks firmly fore and aft,
A sight forlorn. Her decks are all atilt,
Her sheets adrift, her cabin swims in silt.
Her crew, disconsolate upon the bank,
Avow that Fate has played a sorry prank.
" That comes of cutting fine," says Ted, " a lighter
On either side's the only way to right her.

'Taint Luck, 'tis carelessness. A plenty folk
To sail these waters think it just a joke ;
But where the banks are soft, 'tis my belief
You must sail carefully, or come to grief."

Yarmouth, athwart the marshland, in the haze
Of sunset gilded, meets the wanderer's gaze
With beauty unforeseen ; although 'tis true
That Distance lends enchantment to the view !
For soon the Bure becomes a very Styx,
A stream unblessed, where mud and water mix
In league unholy, and on either hand
Battered and grim the scowling houses stand.
A gloomy harbour ; yet the waterside
Where boats and wherries in the night abide
Is trimly tended ; Gordon with his paints
Crouched in the dusk, forgetful of the taints
Which crushed the air ; until the stars came out
And wondered what the lad could be about !

Next morn they tarried till the flood was spent
At low of tide ; then worked their way, content
To leave the muddy Bure, beneath the span
Of Breydon Bridge—high monument of man

The builder, lofty portal of the Yare
By Yarmouth river. And a cloud of care
Vanished away from Ted his honest face.
" Believe me, Breydon is a rare old place
For trouble, since the tides do run so strong
Beneath the bridge, they quickly set you wrong.
And if you chance to get upon the ground,
Why, there you stay, as many an one has found."
On Breydon Water, when the tide is out,
The channel bounds no sailorman can doubt.
Starboard and port, the miry banks reveal
Where safety lies beneath his cautious keel.
But when the Flood has wiped the Water clean,
—Hiding the muddy haunts where seagulls preen
Their oily feathers, and the curlews pipe
A melancholy note, and herons wipe
Their bills, and shake their heads—black pillars mark
The channel's edge for each adventuring bark.
Yet, though a post appear to be in place,
If tack you must, be sure your turning space
Is wide ; the channel shifts, and now and then
A post deceives the hapless wherrymen.

Waveney and Yare, the sister rivers, meet

Beneath an ancient mound ; by Herringfleet,
Beyond Saint Olave's bridge, our company
Sailed on the Waveney's stream ; and all agree
To praise her beauty ; for the bulrush grows
Adown her shores, and every breeze that blows
Ruffles the green and russet regiment.
From flank to flank the unbroken line is bent
And softly whispers as the Wind goes by
Baffled, yet minded new assaults to try.
But all stand stoutly, and the river banks
Are closely shielded 'neath those serried ranks.
Beyond, are meads—and there a distant height
Tree laden, shimmering in the noonday light,
Tells of cool harbourage for those who go
By Somerleyton or by Haddiscoe.

There for a time they made their holiday :
The placid elders chiefly loved to stay
Close to the wherry ; but the boys would take
The boat, and sail away, with fruit and cake
And other meats to comfort them withal.
Oh, heedless Ones, how oft before a fall
Goes Pride ! Yet Youth must be adventuring
With head in air, and lightly take its fling

And make its blunders ; 'tis Experience
Alone begets a cautious common sense.
Despite example, warning, and advice,
They sailed to Breydon Water ; in a trice
The dinghy ran aground ; the tide was high,
Soft was the mud, no mariners were nigh
To bring them succour, on the mud they stayed.
The hours went by ; the dunling whirled and played
About their heads ; with oars they heaved amain
To get them clear ; alas ! the toil was vain.
They broke an oar, they filled the boat with slime,
Till in despair, Jim, frantic but sublime,
Jumped overboard, and miry to the knee
Late and at length availed to set her free.
Meanwhile with anxious brow the elders wait,
Uneasy lest a stroke of pitiless Fate
Has fallen ; oft-times Destiny will smite
When all seems smooth, and scarce beyond our sight
Prepares her torments—ruthless, unforeseen,
Despoiler of the joy that might have been.
So, when the truant wanderers returned,
His fears relieved, with wrath their father burned.
But they, poor wights, with mien apologetic,
Weary, and soiled, and sad, were so pathetic

To the paternal eye, that all his rage

(Though righteous) proved full easy to assuage.

And, as a proof what agonies of soul

Each had endured, their food uneaten, whole

As when they started forth, was found within

The dinghy—absolution for their sin !

Thereafter, sailing when the wind was fair,

They left the Waveney, furrowing the Yare

By Reedham and by Cantley, till they came

Past staithe and marsh to moor at Whitlinghame.

Here by a grassy bank, beneath a wood

Of alder, beech, and sycamore, there stood

An ivy-covered ruin, grey and grim,

Where nightjars shrieked when summer eves grew
    dim.

Was this the spot, a thousand years ago,

Where Saxons fought against the Danish foe

And barred the river to those pirate prows ?

Ah, who can say ! for History allows

Such riddles to be answered as we list,

Half seen, half lost in the enchanted mist

That wraps her birth. Pity that she must grow

Into a damsel colder than the snow,

Clearer than crystal, eloquent as ice,
Severe, relentless, practical, precise.

Enough for them to dream that hereabout
Once men of Norwich put their foes to rout,
And slew a many; but the tawny Dane
Returned, for Saxon folk a bitter bane.
Fancy renewed the strife; on every knoll
The wraiths of shaggy warriors took their toll
Of shadowy foemen, and the longships black
Surged up the stream to aid each wild attack.
And when the dusk was come, and all asleep
The wherry lay, what voice was heard to weep
Out in the night? An owl to make such moan?
'Twas Saxon Ealfred, mourning for his own!

There came a day they turned their ship about
For Yarmouth and the sea, and in and out
And to and fro across the winding Yare
They beat their course. Ted, with a wrinkled stare,
Scowled at the clouds, and when the thunder rolled
Swore soberly; Jim from the dinghy trolled
Astern for pike, but meeting no reward
For all his labour, slowly climbed on board.

A mighty tempest gathered in the North,
Heavy from cavernous mouths to blazon forth
Blind fury, while the crooked lightning thrust
To earth a dazzling shaft ; with fitful gust
The timorous wind stayed for the crack of doom,
And mortals moped and murmured in the gloom.
Down came the rain in rushing cataract ;
Could man conceive a firmament compact
Of sound, of water, and of sudden flame
'Twas here ; a fiery splendour overcame
The comfortable daylight, and the mirth
Of vengeful Titans veiled the sobbing earth.

The tumult ceased. Becalmed the wherry lay,
Though shattered clouds in sombre disarray
Marched in the heavens ; then sudden from the West
The wind roared out ; the waves with foaming crest
Lashed at her side ; she reeled beneath the blow,
Then braced herself against her ancient foe,
Heeled once again, and fled before the blast,
Drooping her peak to ease the groaning mast.
It chanced, a furlong from the Cockatrice
(A lonely alehouse, with a strange device
Upon a painted board) she passed beside

A cargo wherry, drifting on the tide
With blackened sail spread like a broken wing
Half in the water. " Comes o' dallying
With tempests single-handed," quotha Ted.
" Th' old skipper had a son, but—the lad's dead,
Drowned by the Germans off the Dogger Bank
A year agone. His father has to thank
The bloody pirates for the plight he's in,
—A broken gaff to mend, and bread to win
For three grandchildren. Best put in to-night
This side of Reedham, sir, whilst yet 'tis light."
They understood ; made fast, and in the rain
Helped the old man set up his gear again.
Wherry by wherry lay, dim fell the gloaming,
Down came the night. He told of all his roaming
And troubled loneliness ; yet he disdained
To seek their sympathy, and ne'er complained
Against his fate, although the allotted span
Of years was his—a sailor and a man.

Once more they passed through Breydon, to the Bure ;
Escaped the treacherous banks, and lay secure
Moored by the quay. They sailed away at morn
For Potter Heigham and the gentle Thurne.

To Heigham Sound they came, and far away
From all mankind the lonely wherry lay.
The shafted bulrushes, the water weeds,
The floating lilies, and the scented reeds
Embowered her hull in verdant alley ways.
The world around gave to the Maker praise;
Green things in silence, birds with many a cry,
But all united in a minstrelsy
Of patterned worship and fore-ordered prayer.
An harmony filled all the radiant air,
So soft, so delicate, that only those
With hearts attuned to mystery could suppose
The half of it—such ecstacies of sound
Thrilled on the wind. But mortal ears are bound
With fleshly bandage, mortal eyes are slow
In Paradise a Paradise to know.

O peaceful hours ! O peaceful, happy place !
Yet even thou couldst not escape the trace
Of War; beneath the surface of the mere,
Whereon the wherries once might safely steer,
Now surged a clinging weed, a watery grass,
Choking the channel, so that none could pass
On their occasions ; and the guiding posts

Which on a summer's eve, like kindly ghosts,
Beckoned all happy wanderers to the shore,
Were gone from Hickling Broad; for where before
Only the coot and waterfowl took wing,
Seaplanes had clanged and scuttered, hurrying
Down from the clouds, rising in swift ascent,
Roaring defiance at the firmament.
So for long years no keels passed by to scour
The channel clean; in War's ill-omened hour
Foul weeds grow mightily, and day by day
Unchecked they spread, and stopped the water way.

The narrow Ant my venturers essayed
Thereafter to explore, all undismayed
By contrary winds; but as the needle's eye
Is hard for laden camels to pass by,
So is the tenuous Ant a stubborn stream
To sail, without the wind's abaft the beam.
Yet, after weary hours, to Barton Broad
They came at length. But now their precious hoard,
Their store of golden days, was running low :
" To-morrow, back to Wroxham must we go.
Our moon is ended, e'en as all things end,
Our time is spent—we cannot help but spend."

26

So now the enchanted holiday is o'er.
Only from memory's page can men restore
The dear dead hours of yesterday, and soon
In vain we crave for memory's fleeting boon ;
The morning and the evening are as one,
Night comes, and all is said, and all is done.
If for a little while my halting rhyme
Serve to remind you of this wondrous time
Of love renewed, and terror cast away,
'Twill not be penned in vain.

                            I've said my say ;
Children, to bed ; put out the cabin light,
God bless you every one, Good night, Good night.

CPSIA information can be obtained at www.ICGtesting.com
Printed in the USA
LVOW112300070113

314712LV00012B/690/P